DINO DEFENSES

3D DINOSAUR DISCOVERY™

Nodosaurus
(NO-doh-SOR-uhss)

by
Scott Ciencin

with
Matthew T. Carrano, Ph.D.
Consultant

Scholastic Inc.

New York   Toronto   London   Auckland   Sydney
Mexico City   New Delhi   Hong Kong   Buenos Aires

ISBN 0-439-83871-1

Designer: Lee Kaplan

Front cover illustration and title page: *Nodosaurus* © Todd Marshall; (jungle) © Dhoxax/Shutterstock.com.

Back cover illustration: *Centrosaurus* © Jaime Chirinos.

All Ty the *Tyrannosaurus rex* illustrations by Ed Shems.

All 3-D conversions by Pinsharp 3D Graphics.

Photo and Illustration Credits:

Page 5: *Triceratops* © Todd Marshall.

Page 6: *Stegosaurus* © Todd Marshall.

Page 7: (*Triceratops* and *T. rex* museum exhibit) © Charles Shapiro/Shutterstock.com.

Page 8: (*Euoplocephalus*) © Alan Groves; (blue sky) © Karl Naundorf/Shutterstock.com.

Page 9: *Scelidosaurus* © Stephen Missal.

Pages 10–11: *Stegosaurus* © Joe Tucciarone; *Kentrosaurus* © Jaime Chirinos; (fossil *Stegosaurus* plate) © Kris Kripchak.

Page 12: *Therizinosaurus* © Todd Marshall.

Page 13: *Iguanodon* © Todd Marshall.

Pages 14–15: *Styracosaurus* and *Daspletosaurus* © Joe Tucciarone; *Centrosaurus* © Jaime Chirinos.

Page 16: (*Protoceratops* skeleton) © Jim Jurica/Shutterstock.com.

Page 17: *Torosaurus* © Jaime Chirinos (Editor's note: Since grass wasn't around during the Mesozoic, the artist has shown the dinos here on a field of dried-out ferns and low-lying plants.); (*Torosaurus* skull) © Kris Kripchak.

Pages 18–19: *Ankylosaurus* © Todd Marshall; *Shunosaurus* and *Gasosaurus* © John Bindon; (ankylosaur skeleton) © Kris Kripchak; (*Stegosaurus* spike tail) © Kris Kripchak.

Page 20: *Apatosaurus* © Todd Marshall.

Page 21: *Brachiosaurus* © Joe Tucciarone; (cloud forest) © SF Photography/Shutterstock.com.

Page 22–23: *Argentinosaurus* and *Giganotosaurus* © Todd Marshall.

Pages 24–25: *Corythosaurus* © Jaime Chirinos; *Parasaurolophus* © Joe Tucciarone.

Page 26: (Dinosaur trackway) © Anton Wroblewski; *Iguanodon* herd © Todd Marshall.

Page 27: (*Hypsilophodon*) © Alan Groves.

Pages 28–29: (Praying mantis) © Chua Kok Beng Marcus/Shutterstock.com; (polar bear) © Robert St-Coeur/Shutterstock.com; (forest frog) © Alexander M. Omelko/Shutterstock.com; *Zuniceratops* © Todd Marshall.

Page 30: Photo and stegosaur illustration © Ken Carpenter.

Page 31: *Einiosaurus* © Julius Csotonyi; (giant fern) © Doxa/Shutterstock.com; (huge tree) © Dhoxax/Shutterstock.com; (jungle) © Dhoxax/Shutterstock.com.

Page 32: (*Allosaurus* and *Stegosaurus* museum exhibit) © Kris Kripchak.

12 11 10 9 8 7 6 5 4 3   6 7 8 9 10 11/0

Printed in the U.S.A.

First Scholastic printing, March 2006

TABLE OF CONTENTS

WELCOME TO

Welcome back! It's me, Ty! What if you were a plant-eating dino munching on some leaves, and suddenly saw me sneaking up behind you? You might think it's not a big deal since I don't look so scary. But trust me—to a plant-eating dino, meat-eaters like me are reason to be very, very afraid!

So, what's a plant-eater to do when it spots a predator like a *T. rex*? Run? Hide between two big trees, where the *T. rex* can't follow? Or fight back?

Plant-eating dinosaurs used all these ways and more to defend themselves against meat-eaters in order to survive. And it worked—for hundreds of millions of years!

Ty
Tyrannosaurus rex
(tie-RAN-oh-SOR-uhss RECKS)

But what other kinds of **defenses** did these plant-eating dinos have? Did they take karate classes? Nope! Instead…

Dino 🦕 Dictionary

A dino's *defenses* are the things that protect it from predators or other dinos.

◆ Some dinos smacked attackers with special tails!

◆ Some dinos were so big they could stomp on their enemies!

◆ Some dinos sent warning calls through tubes on top of their heads!

Funny Bones

Q: What do you call a dino that never gives up?

A: A *Try*-ceratops!

4

DINO DEFENSES!

A *Triceratops* (try-SER-uh-TOPS) **scares off a hungry predator**

In this book, you'll learn all about how dinos kept themselves safe, and answer some questions like:

◆ What kinds of armor did dinos have?

◆ Why did some dinos travel in big groups?

◆ Could a dino really hide?

 Don't forget—when you see this icon, put on your **3-D glasses** to see the dinos pop!

Ready to become an expert on **dino defenses**? Follow the dinosaur tracks to the next page, and let's get started!

PLAYING IT SAFE

 Stegosaurus (STEG-oh-SOR-uhss)

People have it easy—we can use our brains to come up with ways to protect ourselves from danger. Bad weather outside? Better stay indoors! Feeling chilly? Put on a sweater! Going out on a bike ride? Better wear that helmet!

Yup, you're a smart species!

Dinos, on the other hand, weren't as smart as we are. Lucky for them, they had strong bodies with all sorts of stuff for protection. Although they couldn't build or make things like people can, there were things they could *do* to protect themselves.

The first kinds of defense you'll read about in this book are **physical defenses**. These are special body parts or body features that a dino was born with that helped protect it from predators. Some dinos had bony plates and spikes that worked like armor. Other dinos were safe from predators just because they were so big.

You'll also read about some dinos who used **behavioral defenses**. That means there were things they did to defend themselves and stay safe. You know how you might run away or hide from something scary, or maybe call for help? Dinos did all those things, too!

Turn the page and get ready to explore dino-mite defenses!

A *Triceratops* and *T. rex* museum exhibit

Like dino knights!

Have you ever worn a helmet or padding to protect yourself? Well, some dinos wore their own natural kind of protection (or *armor*) everywhere they went! These armored dinosaurs were members of the **ankylosaur** (ang-KYE-loh-SOR) family.

The armor that protected these dinos were actually small pieces of bone called **scutes** (SKOOTS). Some of these dinos were covered in scutes, making them armored from head to tail! These pieces of bony armor were spaced a bit apart so dinos could move freely. Check out the amazing armored dinos on these two pages!

Dino Dictionary

A *scute* is a small bony plate that grows in a dino's skin. Other reptiles, like turtles and crocs, have scutes, too.

EUOPLOCEPHALUS (YOO-ah-ploh-SEF-uh-lus)
Late Cretaceous—76 million years ago

Euoplocephalus, which was about as big as a minivan (17 feet or 5 m long), had a body like a tank. Its name means "well-armored head," but that wasn't the only part that was armored! Its neck was covered with scutes, and its shoulders were armed with triangular horns. If a meat-eater tried to attack this dino, it would feel like it was swiping its claws against a stone wall! And if the predator still wouldn't leave *Euoplocephalus* alone, it might get the hint after a swipe of its powerful tail (turn to pages 18–20 for more on dino tails!).

Euoplocephalus

SCELIDOSAURUS (skuh-LID-oh-SOR-uhss)

Early Jurassic—185 million years ago

Scelidosaurus was one of the first armored dinos to roam the Mesozoic. About 13 feet (4 m) long, *Scelidosaurus* was covered with big and small scutes to protect it from the meat-eaters of the Early Jurassic. Scientists used to think that *Scelidosaurus* was an early kind of stegosaur (see pages 10–11 for more), but now most think that *Scelidosaurus* was a true ankylosaur.

Scelidosaurus

Great Plates!

Check out the big, flat plates on the back of the dino below. Dinosaurs with plates like these are part of the **stegosaur** (STEG-oh-SOR) family. Scientists used to think that these plates were for protection against dino attacks, but they were made of bone that broke easily. Instead, these plates probably made these dinos seem much larger and harder to kill to predators.

Even though the plates might have broken in a dino battle, stegosaurs had other kinds of protection to help them out. Check out the *Stegosaurus* below to see!

STEGOSAURUS (STEG-oh-SOR-uhss)

Late Jurassic—145 million years ago

This dino was as big as an elephant from trunk to tail, and it had the biggest plates of any stegosaur. The largest plates were as long as a person's arm! Some scientists think that the plates helped keep **Stegosaurus** cool, like an air conditioning system. The dino's blood flowed through the plates and was cooled off by the outside air.

Stegosaurus

Stegosaur **plates** had small grooves for blood vessels that helped the dino keep cool.

Some stegosaurs had small, bony knobs called **ossicles** (OSS-ick-uhls) covering their throats to protect them from a meat-eater's teeth.

Kentrosaurus

Fossil stegosaur plate

KENTROSAURUS (KEN-troh-SOR-uhss)

Late Jurassic—155 million years ago

Another member of the stegosaur family, *Kentrosaurus* was named "spiked lizard" because of the mean-looking spikes that ran down its back and tail. *Kentrosaurus* was smaller than *Stegosaurus*—20 feet (6 m) long—but those spikes were sure to keep predators away!

Some stegosaurs had **spikes** up to 3 feet (1 m) long sticking out from their backs, shoulders, hips, and tails to keep meat-eaters away.

DINO DATA

Usually spikes or plates that pointed sideways or forward were used for defense. Ones that pointed straight up, like stegosaur plates, were just for looks. Scientists figured this out because a predator probably would attack its prey from the sides, not from straight above.

LOOKING SHARP:

No matter how much armor a plant-eater had, sometimes it still wasn't enough to keep a meat-eater away. A meat-eater might not have cared if a dino was armored or covered in plates. It only saw a walking lunch box! But some dinos didn't take this lying down. They had **claws** and **spikes** so they could fight back! Check out these dinos to find out more!

THERIZINOSAURUS
(THER-uh-ZEEN-oh-SOR-uhss)
Late Cretaceous—77 million years ago

As big and heavy as a killer whale, *Therizinosaurus* had the longest and scariest-looking claws of any plant-eating dino ever discovered. Each of its claws was as long as a person's arm! This dino's three-clawed hands were made for tearing tough plants from the ground or pulling branches from trees. They probably also came in handy if *Therizinosaurus* had to defend itself!

Therizinosaurus

DINO DATA

Therizinosaurus was an *omnivore*. That means it ate small animals, like bugs and lizards, as well as plants.

SPIKES AND CLAWS

Iguanodon

IGUANODON (igg-WAHN-no-DON)
Early Cretaceous—110 million years ago

Iguanodon was up to 33 feet (10 m) long—just a little bit bigger than a bulldozer. It had sharp spikes on its hands called "thumb spikes." *Iguanodon* could use these nasty weapons to slash and injure any predator that got too close!

It must be tough to scratch an itch!

HELP WITH HORNS

Wow—don't make these guys angry!

Just like a modern-day rhino uses its horn to defend itself against lions, tigers, and hyenas, many plant-eating dinosaurs had horns, too. Most horned dinos were members of the **ceratopsian** (SER-uh-TOP-see-en) group. These dinos probably fought off hungry predators by charging with their heads down, a bit like rhinos do today.

STYRACOSAURUS (sty-RACK-oh-SOR-uhss)
Late Cretaceous—75 million years ago

Styracosaurus was about 18 feet (5½ m) long and big as a pick-up truck. It had a long horn on its nose that pointed up and out. With its head down, *Styracosaurus*'s horn was just in the right place to get a predator out of its way! This dino was so powerful that its horn could have split the trunk of a small tree! *Styracosaurus* means "spiked lizard" since it had six long spikes on the back edge of its head, which also probably scared off predators.

A group of *Styracosaurus* come face-to-face with a hungry *Daspletosaurus* (das-PLEET-toe-SOR-uhss)

Centrosaurus

CENTROSAURUS (SEN-troh-SOR-uhss)
Late Cretaceous—80 million years ago

Centrosaurus was a little bigger than *Styracosaurus* and also had a long horn on its nose. On some *Centrosaurus*, this horn curved back toward the dino's eyes. On others, it pointed toward its mouth. Any predator who bothered this dino would definitely have been sorry!

DINO DATA

Some dinos were named for the number of horns they had. **Triceratops** (like the one on page 5) had three big horns on its head. *Tri* means "three" and *cerato* means "horn," so *Triceratops* means "three-horned face."

FANCY FRILLS

You might have noticed that the dinos you read about on pages 14–15 also had **frills**—large coverings that started just behind their eyes and swept back over their necks. These frills were made of nearly solid bone that grew from behind the dino's eyes.

What were frills for?

For these dinos, frills helped keep the **backs of their necks safe** from the teeth of meat-eaters. Also, like stegosaur plates, scientists think frills helped these plant-eaters **look much bigger** than they actually were. With this trick, they could scare enemies into backing down without a fight. Read on to discover two dinos who used their frills to the fullest!

PROTOCERATOPS (pro-toe-SER-uh-tops)
Late Cretaceous—85 million years ago

Protoceratops was one dino whose frill made its enemies think twice about attacking it. *Protoceratops* was only about the size of a sheep, but its frill could make it look bigger and more intimidating. While a predator started to change its mind about whether it *really* wanted to take on this dino, *Protoceratops* could escape to safety!

Protoceratops **skeleton**

Torosaurus

TOROSAURUS (TORE-oh-SOR-uhss)
Late Cretaceous—70 million years ago

Torosaurus didn't need a frill to look big—it was big! This dino was up to 25 feet (7½ m) long—as long as an ice-cream truck! Its head alone measured up to 8½ feet (2½ m) long. It probably had one of the biggest heads of any land animal that ever lived!

DINO DATA

Some dinos, like *Protoceratops* and *Torosaurus*, had large holes in their frills. Scientists think these holes may have helped keep the frills from being too heavy for the dinos to hold up.

Torosaurus skull

17

TAIL-TASTIC!

Can you imagine having a tail that you could crack like a whip? How about a tail with a great big hammer on the end? These sure would come in handy if you had to fight a meat-eating dinosaur! Guess what? Some plant-eaters had amazing tails that did just that! Read on to get the scoop on terrific tails!

ANKYLOSAURUS (ang-KYE-loh-SOR-uhss)
Late Cretaceous—65 million years ago

Ankylosaurus was a dino about as long as a school bus, and carried a giant **club tail** (see the next page for more info). With one swing of that club, *Ankylosaurus* might have been able to break a predator's ankles! Stand back!

Ankylosaurus

SHUNOSAURUS (SHOE-noh-SOR-uhss)
Middle Jurassic—175 million years ago

Shunosaurus, a sauropod discovered in China, was on the smaller side for this group of dinos since it was only 33 feet (10 m) long. But *Shunosaurus* made up for its smaller size with a fierce tail that ended in a **spiked club of bone** (can you spot it in the pic below?). You can bet a meat-eater didn't want to be attacked with that tail!

A *Shunosaurus* defends itself against a group of *Gasosaurus* (GAS-oh-SOR-uhss)

Join the Club
Club tails were made of scutes that grew together to form a lump of bone at the end of the dino's tail. The club was strong, but light enough for a dino to swing easily when an enemy got too close.

Ankylosaur skeleton

Stegosaurus spike tail

Yikes, Spikes!
As you read on page 11, dinos like *Stegosaurus* and *Kentrosaurus* had **spike tails** for defense. While club tails were stiff and probably swung like a bat, spike tails were more flexible.

I bet those dinos broke a lot of furniture!

APATOSAURUS (uh-PAT-oh-SOR-uhss)

Late Jurassic—145 million years ago

Apatosaurus was a dino in the **diplodocid** (dip-luh-DAH-kid) family with an unusual kind of tail. Some scientists think that *Apatosaurus* and other diplodocids might have used their long, thin tails like whips to smack a predator when it tried to attack. This dino might have been able to flick its tail so that the end moved faster than the speed of sound, making a loud crack. Ouch!

Apatosaurus

DINO DATA

Scientists now know that diplodocids carried their long, thin tails in the air. They figured this out by looking at how tailbones fit together and the fact that there aren't any drag marks next to fossilized diplodocid footprints.

20

LIVIN' LARGE

Some dinos didn't need sharp claws or fancy frills to make meat-eaters think twice about eating them. That's because they were the **biggest** dinosaurs around!

Who were these big dinos? Many of them were in the **sauropod** (SAW-roh-pod) group—plant-eating dinos with super-long necks and extra-long tails. Sauropods had all sorts of ways of protecting themselves from hungry meat-eaters. The biggest and most important one didn't take a lot of effort. They just had to be themselves: absolutely ENORMOUS!

Brachiosaurus

BRACHIOSAURUS (BRACK-ee-oh-SOR-uhss)
Late Jurassic—145 million years ago

Brachiosaurus was one of the biggest dinosaurs ever. Up to 40 feet (12 m) tall, it could've looked into the fourth-floor window of a skyscraper without a ladder! This dino weighed over 40 tons, more than twice as much as some sauropods. That's as heavy as seven elephants! Its foot was big enough to squish a raptor (a small meat-eating dino) the way you might stomp on a big bug.

Super Size Me!

If a meat-eater about your size leaped out from around a corner, you'd be in big trouble! But what if that meat-eater was **small**—about the size of a guinea pig? As long as it didn't move too fast, you'd have nothing to be afraid of! That's what life was like for sauropods. Most meat-eaters were smaller, so these giant dinos probably didn't worry too much!

Being big was a great defense against pesky meat-eaters. But what if a really brave predator wasn't scared off by a sauropod's big size? These giant dinos had another trick to keep themselves safe!

DINO DATA

Since meat-eaters can get hurt while hunting, predators usually go after smaller prey. If a dino was too big to kill easily, a meat-eater probably stayed away.

Argentinosaurus (are-jen-TEEN-oh-SOR-uhss) **and a pack of** *Giganotosaurus* (JIG-uh-NOTE-oh-SOR-uhss)

Stomping Out Danger

To scare a meat-eater, maybe all a giant sauropod had to do was stomp its feet! Some sauropods were so heavy that they could shake the ground and make most of their enemies scatter. If a stubborn meat-eater still didn't get out of the way, a giant plant-eater could lift a leg and stomp down on its enemy—and squash it!

I think I'll steer clear of sauropods!

23

JUST DO IT!

You've just learned about all sorts of cool body features that protected plant-eaters from their enemies. But even if a dino wasn't big or armored, could it stay safe? You bet! It just had to know what to do. Read on to learn about some of the things that dinos did to protect themselves.

Sound Off!

You might think that big, bad predators did all the roaring in the Mesozoic. But peaceful plant-eaters could make some noise, too. Sudden noises can make anyone jump—even a two-story tall meat-eater! Duckbill dinosaurs called **hadrosaurs** (HAD-roh-sors) used this to their advantage. They made the loudest (and coolest) sounds of the Mesozoic. Check out the two hadrosaurs on these pages!

Yup, it's a dino marching band!

Corythosaurus

CORYTHOSAURUS (core-RITH-oh-SOR-uhss)
Late Cretaceous—80 million years ago

Corythosaurus had a large, hollow **crest** on the top of its head. By blowing air though the crest, scientists think that *Corythosaurus* made trombone-like noises that sounded a lot like a ship's foghorn. By making some noise, *Corythosaurus* could make sure the dinos it was traveling with all stuck together, or it could scare an enemy into backing off.

Dino Dictionary

A *crest* is a horn or ridge on an animal's head. Most of the time crests are for decoration, but sometimes they have special functions, like making noise.

PARASAUROLOPHUS (PAIR-uh-sor-ALL-loh-fuhss)
Late Cretaceous—76 million years ago

Parasaurolophus, a big dino as long as a school bus, made noise with a crest on the top of its head that pointed backward. This crest was longer than a person's leg and totally hollow. Air tubes connected *Parasaurolophus*'s crest to its nose, and the crest vibrated like a trumpet to make noise. The sound could be heard for miles around, and *Parasaurolophus* could warn others in its herd or tell a meat-eater to scram!

Parasaurolophus

Funny Bones

Q: What do you call a dino with earplugs?

A: Anything you want—it can't hear you!

Have You Herd?

Dinosaurs that wanted to avoid danger often traveled in large groups called **herds**. A meat-eater taking on a single dino was one thing, but five or ten? Bad idea! Some herds were made up of one kind of dino, but many herds had different kinds of plant-eating dinosaurs. It was like a dino block party! Sorry Ty, no meat-eaters allowed!

Aw, no fair! I love parties!

Dino trackway near Denver, Colorado

Scientists know that some dinos traveled in herds from studying groups of footprints that stretch over large distances, called dino **trackways**. From these tracks, they can see how many and what kinds of dinos traveled together.

A herd of *Iguanodon*

DINO DATA

From studying dino trackways, scientists have discovered that adults stayed on the outside of the herd and kept the kids on the inside for protection.

A group of *Hypsilophodon*

Run for Cover

If you saw a hungry predator coming your way and there was nowhere to hide, your first thought would probably be to **RUN**! That's what some dinos did, too. Smaller dinosaurs were pros at speeding away from predators. Check out the dino on this page for more info.

HYPSILOPHODON (hip-sill-LOH-foe-don)
Early Cretaceous—115 million years ago

Hypsilophodon was fairly small for a dino—but it could run faster than you can ride a bike! *Hypsilophodon* were lightweight plant-eaters that scientists think had a lot in common with modern gazelles and antelopes (two fast-running creatures alive today). *Hypsilophodon* even had a stiff tail that helped it keep its balance when running. No trips and falls for this dino. That could be deadly!

Ready or Not, Here I Come!

Playing hide-and-seek can be fun—when you *don't* have a hungry *T. rex* on your tail! When you do, hiding could be a matter of life or death!

Many dinos, both big and small, didn't have any way to protect themselves in a fight. The best way they could survive being hunted by predators was to blend in with their surroundings and hide.

Now You See It, Now You Don't!

Dinos with lots of armor, like the *Euoplocephalus* you learned about on page 8, didn't need to hide. In fact, they might even have been brightly colored to warn predators to leave them alone. But dinos that couldn't protect themselves would have wanted to keep meat-eaters from spotting them. One way to stay out of sight was to **hide**. This probably only worked for smaller dinos, though.

Hey...where did I go?

Because skin colors don't last in fossils, scientists don't know what dino skin looked like. But, like many animals today, some dinos probably had **camouflage** (KAM-uh-flahj) that helped them **blend in** when they didn't want to be seen. Look below at the praying mantis on a leaf, the polar bear in the snow, and the forest frog on a tree trunk. Get the idea?

Check out how well ***Zuniceratops*** (ZOO-nee-SER-uh-tops), shown on the next page, blends in with its surroundings. This is just one guess as to what this dino might have looked like. You can see how a meat-eater could miss a dino with this kind of camouflage from far away, since *Zuniceratops* is the same color as the trees around it!

Dino Dictionary

When an animal can blend in with the plants, rocks, or other stuff around it because of markings or coloring on its skin, that's called *camouflage*.

Praying mantis

Polar bear

CAMOUFLAGE

Forest frog

Zuniceratops

Ken Carpenter, a paleontologist at the Denver Museum of Nature & Science, is an expert on dino defenses. Every year, he leads trips to look for dinosaur fossils, usually in the desert of eastern Utah. We caught up with Dr. Carpenter to ask him some questions about dino defenses and other stuff.

Q How did you first become interested in dinosaurs?

A When I was five years old, my mother took me to see the movie *Godzilla: King of the Monsters*. I thought a giant dinosaur stomping around Tokyo was pretty cool, and I decided then that I wanted to study real dinosaurs when I grew up!

Q How old were you when you found your first fossil?

A My very first fossil was a fossil sea urchin that I found in a small cave in Japan when I was in the fifth grade. My first dinosaur discovery, the front leg of a *Stegosaurus*, was found when I was about 16. That fossil is now here in my museum.

Q What do you think is the coolest dinosaur defense?

A The spikes on the end of the *Stegosaurus* tail, because no animal living today has anything like it. Scientists have always thought that those spikes were to keep meat-eating dinosaurs away, but they didn't know for sure. But recently, I've discovered proof! I've found a bone from the tail of the meat-eater *Allosaurus* (AL-oh-SOR-uhss) with a hole in it that matches the spike of *Stegosaurus* perfectly. The hole shows that the bone was infected, which tells me the *Allosaurus* survived the battle with the *Stegosaurus*. Did the infection eventually kill the *Allosaurus*? Maybe. It was certainly a sick animal before it died!

Q What else did *Stegosaurus* have to defend itself with?

A One idea is that the plates on *Stegosaurus*'s back made it look meaner, to keep predators away. *Stegosaurus* might have also scared predators by pumping blood into the skin covering the plates, so that they would look pink. Pink plates would be very noticeable against the green of a forest!

Dr. Carpenter created this picture of two stegosaurs on his computer

Einiosaurus

EINIOSAURUS

Discovered in Montana, this dino was a plant-eater that lived in the Late Cretaceous (about 74 million years ago). Because of its body shape, its name comes from the Blackfoot Indian word for "buffalo." While buffaloes grow to about 10 feet long (3 m), *Einiosaurus* (eye-NEE-oh-SOR-uhss) was twice that size!

The truly weird-looking *Einiosaurus* probably wouldn't have liked being called "can-opener nose"—but its horned nose, which curved forward, did look like a giant can opener! And like other horned dinosaurs, *Einiosaurus* could hook and tear with its horn, making it a fierce enemy in any fight.

Einiosaurus's horn probably had other uses aside from keeping this plant-eater safe from predators. Like many other ceratopsians, *Einiosaurus* spent most of its time eating or wandering around looking for food, so its horn may have helped it to dig up tough plants on the ground. It may also have helped other *Einiosaurus* to recognize that it was an *Einiosaurus*, too.

MORE DINO ADVENTURES COMING SOON!

We're at the end of our adventure exploring dino defenses! We've seen the many ways dinos defended themselves, from dino armor to squashing predators with their feet, and even meeting a full-on attack with claws, spikes, or a fierce tail. But there's still lots more to explore in the world of dinos! See you soon for another exciting step—or *stomp*—back in time!

Museum exhibit showing an *Allosaurus* attacking two *Stegosaurus*